50 Decadent
Cake Frosting And Filling
Recipes

By
Brenda Van Niekerk

ISBN-13:978-1505673395
ISBN-10:1505673399

Content

Nougat Frosting

Ingredients

10 ml gelatin
125 ml cold water
250 ml butter
50 ml icing sugar
397 g condensed milk
5 ml vanilla extract
5 ml ream of tartar
Pinch salt
2 ml almond extract
5 ml lemon extract
250 ml glace fruit
125 ml almonds (chopped)

Method

Sprinkle the gelatin over the cold water and soak until spongy.

Melt over a low heat.

Cream the butter and icing sugar together.

Add the gelatin.

Add the condensed milk, vanilla extract, cream of tartar, salt, almond extract and lemon extract.

Mix well.

Add the glace fruit and almonds.

Mix well and chill until set.

Chocolate Frosting

Ingredients

25 ml cocoa powder
25 ml hot milk
12,5 ml margarine
300 ml icing sugar
2 ml vanilla extract

Method

Blend cocoa powder and milk until smooth.

Beat in the margarine.

Added icing sugar and vanilla extract.

Beat until creamy.

Honey Cardamom Butter Cream

Ingredients

250 ml butter
100 ml honey
1000 ml icing sugar
5 ml ground cardamom
 25 ml cream

Method

Cream the butter and honey together.

Add the icing sugar and cardamom.

Beat until smooth and creamy.

Add the cream and beat for 2 minutes.

Pistachio And Lemon Frosting

Ingredients

125 g icing sugar
25 ml lemon juice
60 g pistachio nuts (chopped)

Method

Blend icing sugar with lemon juice.

Add the pistachio nuts.

Butterscotch Frosting

Ingredients

30 g butter

30 ml brown sugar

30 ml evaporated milk

Method

Place all the ingredients into a saucepan and heat until the sugar has melted.

Bring to boil and stop stirring, boil for 10 to 15 minutes.

Pour over cake immediately.

Boiled Icing

Ingredients

100 g margarine
280 g icing sugar
25 ml milk

Method

Melt margarine in a saucepan.

Heat milk separately.

Remove the margarine from the heat and then add the milk and 140 g icing sugar.

Stir well and return to the heat.

Bring to boil without stirring.

As soon as the mixture boils remove from the heat and stir in the remaining icing sugar.

Blend well.

Work quickly as icing hardens.

Flavor and color as desired.

Fudge Frosting

Ingredients

60 g margarine
40 g dark chocolate
500 ml icing sugar
90 ml milk
5 ml vanilla extract
1 ml salt

Method

Melt margarine and chocolate over low heat.

Remove from heat and add icing sugar, milk, vanilla extract and salt.

Mix thoroughly.

Coffee Cream

Ingredients

25 g butter
5 ml vanilla extract
250 ml icing sugar
10 ml instant coffee powder
10 ml hot water
10 ml milk

Method

Beat butter and vanilla extract together until creamy.

Add icing sugar until well combined.

Dissolve coffee powder and hot water.

Allow the mixture to cool.

Add the coffee mixture to the butter mixture with the milk.

Mix well.

Peanut Butter Cream Frosting

Ingredients

500g icing sugar
25 ml milk
1 ml vanilla extract
125 g margarine
125 g peanut butter

Method

Beat the margarine and peanut butter together.

Add half the icing sugar and the milk.

Blend well together.

Add the rest of the icing sugar and the vanilla extract.

Pumpkin Pie Butter Cream

Ingredients

250 ml butter
750 ml icing sugar
2 ml powdered ginger
2 ml ground cloves
2 ml ground nutmeg
2 ml cinnamon
3 ml vanilla extract
25 ml milk

Method

Beat the butter, spices and icing sugar together for 2 minutes.

Add the vanilla extract and milk.

Chocolate Whisky Ganache

Ingredients

230 grams dark chocolate
187 ml cream
30 g butter
10 ml Irish Whisky

Method

Melt the chocolate and cream over hot water.

Add the butter and whiskey.

Blend well.

Set aside to cool slightly.

Chocolate Ganache

Ingredients

> 230 g dark chocolate
> 187 ml cream
> 10 ml rum

Method

Melt the chocolate and cream over hot water.

Add the rum.

Blend well.

Set aside to cool slightly.

White Chocolate Ganache

Ingredients

230 g white chocolate
187 ml cream

Method

Melt the chocolate and cream over hot water.

Blend well.

Set aside to cool slightly.

Treacle Frosting

Ingredients

50 g butter
12,5 ml black treacle
12,5 ml milk
225 g icing sugar

Method

Beat all the ingredients together until smooth.

Cream Cheese Frosting

Ingredients

10 oz cream cheese
14 oz icing fondant
7 oz shortening

Method

Beat the cream cheese and icing fondant together until smooth.

Add the shortening.

Mix until smooth and light.

Passion Fruit Frosting

Ingredients

      4 passion fruit (pulp and juice)
      9 oz mascarpone
      12, 5 ml caster sugar
      5 ml vanilla extract
      7 oz fromage frais

Method

Combine the mascarpone, fromage frais, sugar and vanilla extract together.

Fold in the passion fruit.

Brown Sugar Frosting

Ingredients

50 ml butter
20 ml brown sugar
500 ml icing sugar
10 ml vanilla extract
50 ml boiling water

Method

Heat the butter and brown sugar in a saucepan until the sugar has dissolved.

Remove from heat and add the icing sugar.

Add the vanilla extract.

Add the boiling water a little at a time until the frosting is the right consistency.

Lemon Ginger Frosting

Ingredients

50 ml condensed milk
5 ml lemon juice
250 ml icing sugar (sifted)
2 ml ground ginger

Method

Combine the condensed milk and lemon juice together.

Add the icing sugar and ginger.

Mix until smooth.

Pink Rose Frosting

Ingredients

25 g butter
5 ml rose water
250 ml icing sugar
20 ml milk
Few drops pink food coloring
125 ml crushed dry rose petals

Method

Beat the butter and rose water together until creamy.

Add icing sugar until well combined.

Add the milk.

Mix well.

Add a few drops of pink coloring and mix well.

Stir in the crushed rose petals.

French Butter Cream

Ingredients

    12 oz sugar
    3 oz water
    4.5 oz egg yolks
    15 oz butter
    Pinch salt
    7,5 ml vanilla extract

Method

Bring the sugar and water to the boil.

Cover the saucepan and boil for 3 minutes.

Remove the lid and cook the sugar to 240 F.

Beat the egg yolks and salt until light and fluffy.

Remove syrup from heat and slowly pour into egg mixture whisking all the time.

Whisk at high speed until the mixture is cool.

Beat in the butter.

Add the vanilla extract.

Cardamom And Orange Butter Cream

Ingredients

125 ml shortening
125 ml butter
5 ml ground cardamom
1000 ml icing sugar
25 ml orange juice

Method

Cream shortening and butter until light and fluffy.

Add ground cardamom and mix well.

Gradually add icing sugar, one cup at a time.

Blend well on medium speed.

Add orange juice and beat until light and fluffy.

Lemon Verbena Frosting

Ingredients

125 ml shortening
125 ml butter
125 ml minced fresh lemon verbena leaves
1000 ml icing sugar
25 ml milk

Method

Cream shortening and butter until light and fluffy.

Wash the lemon verbena leaves and mince finely in a food processor.

Add the minced lemon verbena leaves to the butter mixture and mix well.

Gradually add icing sugar, one cup at a time.

Blend well on medium speed.

Add the milk and beat until light and fluffy.

Honey And Chocolate Butter Cream

Ingredients

 250 ml butter
 100 ml honey
 875 ml icing sugar
 125 ml cocoa powder
  25 ml cream

Method

Cream the butter and honey together.

Add the icing sugar and cocoa powder.

Beat until smooth and creamy.

Add the cream and beat for 2 minutes.

Lemon And Lavender Frosting

Ingredients

50 ml condensed milk
5 ml lemon juice
250 ml icing sugar (sifted)
75 ml crushed dried lavender flowers

Method

Combine the condensed milk and lemon juice together.

Add the icing sugar.

Mix until smooth.

Add the lavender flowers and mix well.

Cherry Butter Cream

Ingredients

125 ml shortening
125 ml butter
1000 ml icing sugar
25 ml maraschino cherry juice
Few drops pink food coloring
100 ml chopped maraschino cherries

Method

Cream shortening and butter until light and fluffy.

Gradually add icing sugar, one cup at a time.

Blend well on medium speed.

Add the maraschino cherry juice and beat until light and fluffy.

Add a few drops of pink food coloring and the chopped cherries.

Vanilla And Saffron Meringue Frosting

Ingredients

3 egg whites
187 ml sugar
2 ml salt
83 ml water
5 ml vanilla extract
5 ml saffron

Method

Beat the egg whites and sugar with an electric beater until stiff.

Add the salt, vanilla extract and water.

Add the saffron.

Continue beating 4 or 5 minutes until the frosting is the right consistency.

Honey And Walnut Frosting

Ingredients

468 ml honey
3 egg whites
2 ml teaspoon salt
7,5 ml vanilla extract
100 ml walnuts (chopped)

Method

Heat the honey slightly.

Beat the egg white, salt and vanilla extract with an electric beater until stiff.

Add the honey and continue beating for about 10 minutes until mixture has the right consistency.

Mix in the walnuts.

Maple And Brandy Frosting

Ingredients

125 ml shortening
125 ml butter
1000 ml icing sugar
12,5 ml brandy
12,5 ml maple syrup

Method

Cream shortening and butter until light and fluffy.

Gradually add icing sugar, one cup at a time.

Blend well on medium speed.

Add the brandy and maple syrup and beat until light and fluffy.

Mandarin Frosting

Ingredients

125 ml shortening
125 ml butter
1000 ml icing sugar
25 ml mandarin juice
Zest of 1 mandarin

Method

Cream shortening and butter until light and fluffy.

Gradually add icing sugar, one cup at a time.

Blend well on medium speed.

Add the mandarin juice and mandarin zest and beat until light and fluffy.

Orange Filling

Ingredients

100 ml orange juice
25 ml water
25 ml lemon juice
15 ml corn flour
60 g sugar
1 egg (well beaten)
Zest on 1 orange
15 ml butter

Method

Place the fruit juice in a saucepan and bring to boil.

Mix the sugar, corn flour and a little of the warm fruit juice to make a paste.

Add the corn flour mixture to the saucepan and cook until mixture has thickened.

Add the egg.

Stir and allow the mixture to simmer for 1 minute.

Add the zest and butter.

Mix well.

Lemon Filling

Ingredients

125 ml lemon juice
Zest of 1 lemon
50 ml water
15 ml corn flour
60 g sugar
1 egg (well beaten)
15 ml butter

Method

Place the fruit juice in a saucepan and bring to boil.

Mix the sugar, corn flour and a little of the warm fruit juice to make a paste.

Add the corn flour mixture to the saucepan and cook until mixture has thickened.

Add the egg.

Stir and allow the mixture to simmer for 1 minute.

Add the zest and butter.

Mix well.

Cream Filling

Ingredients

    125 g margarine
    90 g cream cheese
    25 ml instant vanilla pudding mix
    250 ml icing sugar
    25 ml milk

Method

Cream margarine, cream cheese and vanilla pudding mix.

Beat in icing sugar and milk.

Blueberry Cream Cheese Filling

Ingredients

> 250 ml butter
> 8 oz cream cheese
> 1,2 oz blueberries (pureed)
> Approximately 4 cups of cups of icing sugar

Method

Beat the butter and cream cheese together.

Add the blueberries.

Add 3 cups of icing sugar and mix.

Add the 4th cup of icing sugar slowly and only if necessary.

Tiramisu Filling

Ingredients

6 eggs
250 ml caster sugar
500 g Mascarpone

Method

Beat the egg yolks with the sugar for 15 minutes.

Add the mascarpone.

Beat until smooth and creamy.

Coffee And Van Der Hum Filling

Ingredients

125 ml butter
4 egg yolks
750 ml icing sugar
20 ml strong coffee powder
20 ml cocoa powder
Pinch cinnamon
25 ml Van Der Hum liqueur

Method

Cream the butter and egg yolks together.

Add the icing sugar and beat well.

Combine the coffee powder, cinnamon, cocoa powder and liqueur together to form a paste.

Add the coffee paste to the butter mixture.

Beat well.

Chill for 10 minutes.

Chocolate Cream Filling

Ingredients

250 ml cream
375 ml icing sugar
200 ml cocoa powder
10 ml vanilla extract
5 ml gelatin
25 ml cold water

Method

Whip the cream until stiff.

Beat in the icing sugar and the cocoa powder.

Chill in the refrigerator for 1 hour.

Soak the gelatin in the cold water over a bowl of boiling water.

Allow the gelatin to cool once the gelatin has dissolved.

Beat the gelatin into the icing mixture.

Ginger Filling

Ingredients

> 250 ml golden syrup
> 250 ml boiling water
> 2 ml ground ginger
> 50 ml ginger preserve (chopped up)
> 30 ml corn flour
> 15 ml custard powder

Method

Heat the syrup, water and the ground ginger to boiling point.

Add the ginger preserve.

Combine the corn flour and custard powder with a little cold water and mix to make a paste.

Add to the syrup mixture and cook for 3 minutes, stirring continuously.

Use on cake while warm.

Lemongrass Butter Cream

Ingredients Lemongrass Milk

187 ml milk
1/2 lemongrass stalk (sliced)

Ingredients Butter Cream

125 ml shortening
125 ml butter
1000 ml icing sugar
25 ml lemongrass milk

Method

Lemongrass Milk

Boil the milk and lemongrass for 3 minutes.

Remove from heat and allow the milk mixture to cool.

Pour into a blender and blend for a minute.

Allow the lemongrass milk to cool fully before using.

Butter Cream

Cream shortening and butter until light and fluffy.

Gradually add icing sugar, one cup at a time.

Blend well on medium speed.

Add the lemongrass milk and beat until light and fluffy.

Lemongrass, Kaffir Lime And Coconut Frosting

Ingredients

125 ml shortening
125 ml butter
1000 ml icing sugar
25 ml coconut milk
1 1/2 lemongrass stalks
3 Kaffir Lime leaves (washed)

Method

Place the lemongrass stalks and Kaffir lime leaves into a blender and mince finely.

Cream shortening and butter until light and fluffy.

Gradually add icing sugar, one cup at a time.

Blend well on medium speed.

Add the coconut milk and beat until light and fluffy.

Add 5 ml of lemongrass / Kaffir lime paste and mix well.

Espresso Butter Cream

Ingredients

125 ml shortening
125 ml butter
975 ml icing sugar
25 ml milk
25ml espresso powder

Method

Cream shortening and butter until light and fluffy.

Gradually add the icing sugar and espresso powder.

Blend well on medium speed.

Add the milk and beat until light and fluffy.

Sour Cream And Coconut Frosting

Ingredients

125 ml shortening
125 ml butter
1000 ml icing sugar
25 ml sour cream
5 ml coconut extract

Method

Cream shortening and butter until light and fluffy.

Gradually add the icing sugar.

Blend well until fluffy on medium speed.

Add the sour cream and coconut extract and beat until light and fluffy.

Chocolate Orange Liqueur Frosting

Ingredients

25 ml cocoa powder
25 ml orange liqueur
12,5 ml margarine
300 ml icing sugar
5 ml orange zest

Method

Blend the cocoa powder and the orange liqueur until smooth.

Beat in the margarine.

Continue beating with an electric beater until the mixture is light and fluffy.

Add the icing sugar and orange zest.

Mix well.

Coffee Liqueur Frosting

Ingredients

125 ml shortening
125 ml butter
975 ml icing sugar
25 ml coffee powder
10 ml milk
20 ml coffee liqueur

Method

Cream shortening and butter until light and fluffy.

Gradually add the icing sugar and the coffee powder.

Blend well until fluffy on medium speed.

Add the milk and coffee liqueur.

Mix well.

Limoncello Liqueur Frosting

Ingredients

125 ml shortening
125 ml butter
1000 ml icing sugar
25 ml Limoncello liqueur
5 ml lemon zest

Method

Cream shortening and butter until light and fluffy.

Gradually add the icing sugar and the lemon zest.

Blend well until fluffy on medium speed.

Add the Limoncello liqueur.

Mix well.

Beer Frosting

Ingredients

125 ml shortening
125 ml butter
1000 ml icing sugar
25 ml stout
5 ml vanilla extract

Method

Cream shortening and butter until light and fluffy.

Gradually add the icing sugar.

Blend well until fluffy on medium speed.

Add the vanilla extract and the stout.

Mix well.

Root Beer Frosting

Ingredients

3 egg whites
187 ml sugar
2 ml salt
78 ml water
10 ml root beer concentrate

Method

Beat the egg whites and sugar with an electric beater until stiff.

Add the salt, root beer concentrate and water.

Continue beating 4 or 5 minutes until the frosting is the right consistency.

Chocolate Malt Frosting

Ingredients

> 125 ml shortening
> 125 ml butter
> 750 ml icing sugar
> 125 ml malted milk powder
> 125 ml cocoa powder
> 25 ml milk
> 5 ml vanilla extract

Method

Cream shortening and butter until light and fluffy.

Gradually add the icing sugar, malted milk powder and cocoa powder.

Blend well until fluffy on medium speed.

Add the vanilla extract and the milk.

Mix well.

Pecan And Rum Butter Cream

Ingredients

125 ml shortening
125 ml butter
1000 ml icing sugar
25ml milk
10 ml rum
125 ml pecan nuts (chopped)

Method

Cream shortening and butter until light and fluffy.

Gradually add the icing sugar.

Blend well until fluffy on medium speed.

Add the rum and the milk.

Add the pecan nuts.

Mix well.

Chocolate Macadamia Ricotta Frosting

Ingredients

750 ml ricotta cheese
312 ml icing sugar
10 ml vanilla extract
62,5 ml cocoa powder
250 ml macadamia nuts (chopped)

Method

Combine the ricotta cheese, icing sugar, vanilla extract and cocoa powder.

Beat the mixture with an electric mixer until smooth and fluffy.

Add the macadamia nuts.

Eggnog Butter Cream

Ingredients

125 ml eggnog
7,5 ml ground cinnamon
3 ml grated nutmeg
1 lb icing sugar
2 ml salt
2 sticks butter
125 ml shortening

Method

Use an electric beater and blend the icing sugar, eggnog, salt, cinnamon and nutmeg together.

Beat in the butter.

Add the shortening and whip at highest speed 10 minutes.

17294949R00032

Printed in Great Britain
by Amazon